I'll Pass for Your Comrade

★ ★ ★ ★ ★ ★ ★ ★ ★ ★ ★ ★ ★ ★ ★ ★ ★ ★ ★

I'll Pass for Your Comrade

WOMEN SOLDIERS IN THE CIVIL WAR

★ ★ ★ ★ ★ ★ ★ ★ ★ ★ ★ ★ ★ ★ ★ ★

Anita Silvey

Clarion Books ★ New York

Clarion Books
an imprint of Houghton Mifflin Harcourt Publishing Company
215 Park Avenue South, New York, NY 10003
Copyright © 2008 by Anita Silvey

The text was set in 12-point Meridien Roman.
Book design by Michelle Gengaro.
Maps by Kayley LeFaiver.

www.clarionbooks.com

Printed in the U.S.A.

Library of Congress Cataloging-in-Publication Data
Silvey, Anita.
I'll pass for your comrade : women soldiers in the Civil War / by Anita Silvey.
p. cm.
Includes bibliographical references and index.
ISBN: 978-0-618-57491-9
1. Women soldiers—United States—History—19th century—Juvenile literature.
2. Women soldiers—Confederate States of America—History—19th century—Juvenile
literature. 3. Women—United States—History—19th century—Juvenile literature.
4. Women—Confederate States of America—History—Juvenile literature.
5. United States—History—Civil War, 1861–1865—Participation, Female—Juvenile
literature. 6. United States—History—Civil War, 1861–1865—Women—Juvenile
literature. I. Title.
E628.S555 2008
973.7'4082—dc22   2008018053

MP   10 9 8 7 6 5 4 3 2 1

To Harold T. Miller,
mentor and friend,
for all his encouragement
and help with this book

★ ★ ★ ★ ★ ★ ★ ★ ★ Contents ★ ★ ★ ★ ★ ★ ★ ★ ★

★ ★

At noon the battle [First Battle of Bull Run] was at its fiercest, and the scene was grand beyond description. The simile that came into my mind was the great Desert of Sahara, with a broiling sun overhead, and immense whirlwinds of sand rolling along over the plain between heaven and earth. The red dust from the parched and sun-dried roads arose in clouds in every direction, while the smoke from the artillery and musketry slowly floated aloft in huge, fantastic columns. . . . It was a sight never to be forgotten,—one of those magnificent spectacles that cannot be imagined. . . . I would not have missed it for the wealth of the world, and was more than repaid for all that I had undergone, and all the risks to my person and my womanly reputation that I incurred, in being not only a spectator, but an actor, in such a sublime, living drama.

—Loreta Janeta Velazquez
The Woman in Battle
[about her participation as a soldier
in the First Battle of Bull Run]

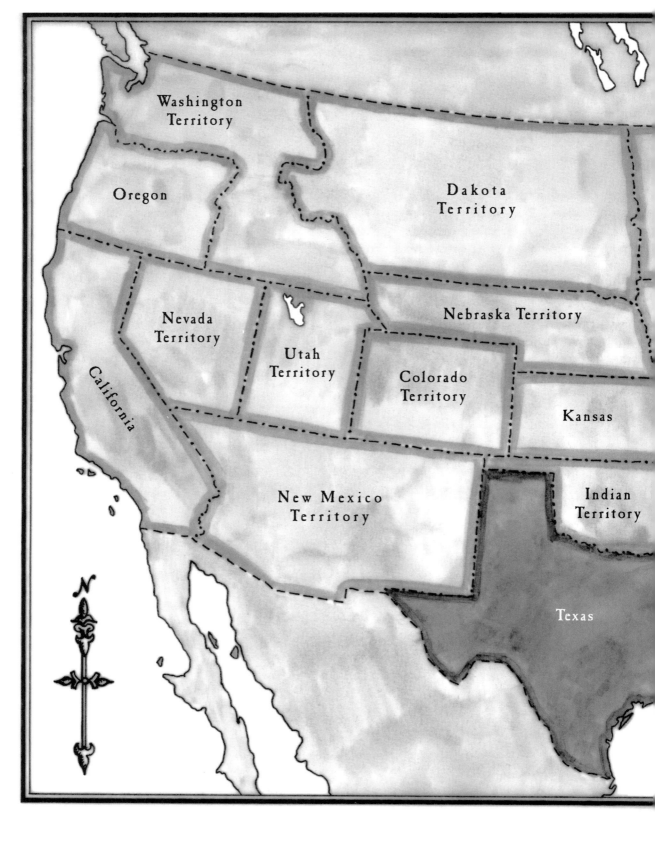

The
UNITED STATES
IN 1861

Minnesota
Wisconsin
Michigan
Maine
Vermont
New Hampshire
Massachusetts
New York
Rhode Island
Connecticut
Pennsylvania
New Jersey
Delaware
Maryland
Iowa
Illinois
Indiana
Ohio
Missouri
Virginia
Kentucky
North Carolina
Tennessee
South Carolina
Arkansas
Mississippi
Alabama
Georgia
Louisiana
Florida

The 11 Confederate states

K. LeFaiver

Loreta Janeta Velazquez, disguised as Lieutenant Harry T. Buford, heads out to join the Confederate army. Steel engraving by an unknown artist from her book, *The Woman in Battle*, published in 1876.

1

"The music of regimental bands"

The First Battle of Bull Run

★ ★

For the First Battle of Bull Run, the first major confrontation of the American Civil War, Northern and Southern troops descended on a small Virginia town, Manassas Junction, near a meandering creek called Bull Run. As they passed through towns along the way, both sides were feted with patriotic parades, and most of the soldiers eagerly awaited their engagement with the enemy.

Among them marched a Confederate officer known as Lieutenant Harry T. Buford. Harry, in real life Loreta Janeta

Velazquez, had constructed an elaborate costume to disguise herself as a man and a soldier. She was elated

> at the prospect before me of being able to prove myself as good a fighter as any of the gallant men who had taken up arms in behalf of the cause of Southern independence. I had only one fear, and that was that I should be stopped on account of not having the proper

Sunday afternoon, July 21, 1861: The Union army flees during the First Battle of Bull Run. Print by J. Brown, around 1861.

Battle scenes from the First Battle of Bull Run.
Hand-colored lithograph by H. H. Lloyd, around 1861.

papers; but my motto was, "Nothing venture, nothing have."

Other soldiers, however, already had a sense of the seriousness of the battle that was about to begin. Sarah Emma Edmonds, disguised as a man named Franklin Thompson, marched into battle as a Union soldier with different emotions that day. She later recalled:

> In gay spirits the army moved forward, the air resounding with the music of regimental bands, the patriotic songs of the soldiers. . . . I felt strangely out of harmony with the wild, joyous spirit which pervaded the troops. . . . I thought that many, very many, of those enthusiastic men who appeared so eager to meet the enemy, would never return to relate the success or defeat of that splendid army.

In that one day, July 21, 1861, Confederate deaths numbered around 2,000; Union deaths, 3,000. The army in blue (the North) and the army in gray (the South) would go on to fight for four more years, a long and brutal conflict that took place at some 10,000 sites and left 620,000 soldiers dead. The history and details of the Civil War—so grisly in its fighting, so important in the history of the United States—have been related in thousands of books, movies, television specials, songs, and articles. But one fact about that war has rarely been mentioned until recently.

Like Loreta Janeta Velazquez and Sarah Emma Edmonds, hundreds of women disguised themselves as men so they could fight as soldiers.

Cover illustration for sheet music of a Civil War ballad, "Good Bye, Sweetheart." Some women were unwilling to be parted from loved ones and joined them in the ranks.

2

"Won't you let me come with you?"
Reasons for Becoming a Soldier

★ ★

*W*hen the citizens of a nation declare war on their fellow citizens, there is never one single, simple reason. However, in America's Civil War, which began in 1861 and lasted into 1865, one issue was definitely at the heart of the conflict. The two sides, the North and the South, disagreed about which governing body—the federal (national) government or the individual state governments—held the ultimate power and could determine policy.

There were profound cultural and economic differences between the two adversaries. Most people in the South, where slavery was prevalent, believed that America's four million slaves were necessary for the nation's economic

The Cruel War
A Civil War Ballad

The cruel war is raging, Johnny has to fight.
I long to be with him from morning till night.
I want to be with him, it grieves my heart so—
Won't you let me come with you? No, my love, no.

Tomorrow is Sunday, Monday is the day
that your captain will call you and you must obey.
Your captain will call you, it grieves my heart so—
Won't you let me come with you? No, my love, no.

I'll tie back my hair, men's clothing I'll put on.
I'll pass for your comrade as we march along.
I'll pass for your comrade, no one will ever know—
Won't you let me come with you? No, my love, no.

Oh Johnny, oh Johnny, I feel you are unkind.
I love you far better than all of mankind.
I love you far better than words can e'er express.
Won't you let me come with you? Yes, my love, yes.

survival. Many in the North insisted that slavery was immoral and should be abolished. The two sides even disagreed, and continue to do so, about the name of the war, known in the North as the Civil War and in the South as the War Between the States.

After the election of Abraham Lincoln to the presidency in 1861, eleven Southern states seceded, or officially withdrew, from the United States of America and formed the Confederate States of America. Supporters of the Confederacy believed that since Lincoln seemed to be allied with Northern interests—unsympathetic to slaveholders and to the authority of individual states—they could simply dissolve the country and form another one. Those on the side of the North, known as the Union, insisted that states could not withdraw and create their own entity. Both the Southern Rebels and the Northern Yankees were willing to fight and die to defend their points of view. President Lincoln called for individuals to enlist as soldiers for the Union. Both sides believed that the conflict would last no more than ninety days.

Once the war had begun, both women and men searched for ways to serve the Union and the Confederacy. Although men were expected to enlist, any woman who actively participated in the Civil War was an oddity if not a renegade. In the 1860s Americans held extremely rigid ideas about what women could and should do. Men concerned themselves with the outside world; women raised children and took care of the home. A woman needed to appear submissive, modest, religious, and focused on family and home. She did not have the right to seek an education; she had few opportunities for paid work and generally could be employed only as a domestic servant—taking care of children, cooking, and cleaning house. A married woman had no legal rights, could not own property, and could not appear in court. Women could not vote. Any woman who ventured out of the home to Civil War battlefields would have been considered abnormal.

Women who volunteered to serve often faced immediate rejection by governmental agencies. A group of more than twenty women in the Shenandoah Valley of Virginia wrote to the Confederate Secretary of War stating that they had organized a volunteer regiment and wanted to play a part in the conflict. The Secretary of War politely declined their offer. All across the North—in cities such as Providence, New York, Philadelphia, and Cleveland—black women volunteered to serve "as nurses, seamstresses, and warriors if need be." Local officials refused their services, both because of their race and because of their sex.

A few women, usually through persistence, found acceptable ways to take part in the war effort: Dorothea Dix organized the Union's army nurses for four years without pay; Mary Livermore headed the Union's Sanitary Commission, inspecting army camps and hospitals. Elizabeth Van Lew, Rose O'Neal Greenhow, and Belle Boyd served as spies. Scores of others, like Clara Barton, volunteered to be nurses. These women achieved some fame and recognition for their

**Clara Barton, the most famous nurse of the Civil War,
photographed by Mathew Brady during the war.**

efforts and are frequently mentioned in accounts of the Civil War.

If a woman wanted to be close to the troops and military action, she might be able to secure one of the few positions available for her. A "daughter of the regiment" encouraged and provided moral support for male comrades in military exercise, in camp, and in battle. A kind of female mascot, certainly not as respected as a soldier, the daughter of the regiment could still get caught in battle skirmishes. Kady Brownell had tried to enlist in the 1st Rhode Island Infantry with her husband but was turned back by a commander. She stayed on as a daughter of the regiment and saw a great deal of action in battle.

Other women helped soldiers by providing needed services,

Civil War photograph of Kady Brownell in the uniform she wore as a daughter of the regiment for the 1st Rhode Island Infantry.

such as being laundresses or supplying the troops with tobacco, food, and other goods—a position called a "sutler" or "vivandiere." Marie Tepe (or Tebe), who was known as "French Mary," traveled with the Pennsylvania 27th and 114th, supplying special provisions and often washing, cleaning, and sewing for the soldiers. A woman of great courage, she aided wounded soldiers during some of the worst fighting of the war.

Laundresses carried washtubs and soap from camp to

Civil War photograph of Marie Tepe, called "French Mary," in her uniform.

camp and cleaned uniforms. A slave named Susie Baker King was freed by Union forces when they arrived on St. Simons Island, Georgia. As a laundress she began traveling with the 1st South Carolina Volunteers, a unit composed of former slaves. She learned to handle a musket and often came under fire when she was close to battle lines.

Some women didn't want to support the troops; they longed to be part of the troops. Even though no one expected them to fight or wanted them to fight, they became soldiers.

What would prompt a woman to defy social convention and put her life in danger by going to war? For some it was a passionate belief in the cause of either the Union or the Confederacy. Emily, a Union sympathizer whose last name remains unknown, was a native of Brooklyn, New York, and enlisted in 1863 at the age of nineteen. She

Susie King (later Taylor) worked as a laundress for the 1st South Carolina volunteers. A halftone photograph from her autobiography, *Reminiscences of My Life in Camp*, published in 1902.

believed that "Providence had destined her . . . to marshal our discouraged forces, rally them to new efforts, and inspire them with a fresh and glowing enthusiasm." While visiting an aunt, Emily dressed up as a man and enlisted in a Michigan regiment. She fought in the Battle of Chicka-mauga, Tennessee, where she was mortally wounded. She reportedly died saying, "I expected to deliver my country but the Fates would not have it so." (Such flowery formal language in solemn moments was conventional at the time.)

Sarah Emma Edmonds, born in New Brunswick, Canada, enjoyed a rugged outdoor life, grew strong working on a farm, and loved to hunt and fish. When her father wanted

"Riding for Life," an illustration from **Sarah Emma Edmonds's memoir,** *Nurse and Spy in the Union Army,* **1864. Wood engraving by R. O'Brien.**

her to marry an aging farmer, Sarah ran away, eventually disguising herself as a man, Franklin Thompson, to keep her father from finding her. She sold Bibles door to door and traveled around New Brunswick and Nova Scotia.

Eager for more adventure, Edmonds, still in disguise, moved to Flint, Michigan, in 1860. In May 1861 she and a male friend enlisted in the 2nd Michigan Voluntary Infantry. She felt she "could best serve the interest of the Union cause in male attire." Much of the time she worked in a medical capacity, nursing the wounded, and she also carried mail. But she suspended these duties to fight in some of the fiercest battles of the war.

As the ballad "The Cruel War" suggests, women frequently entered the ranks to be near a loved one—a husband, sweetheart, or brother. These women tended to receive favorable press when their stories became public because they became soldiers "for the love of a man," a motivation that gained the sympathy of the all-male press corps. Consequently, we know a good deal more about them than we do about the women who had other reasons for joining the army.

When William Lindley enlisted in the 6th U.S. Cavalry, his wife, Martha Parks Lindley, did not want to be left behind. Wearing clothes of his, she joined his regiment under the alias Jim Smith. Although she told the recruiter that she had been a soldier, she was actually a mother who was leaving her two children behind with her sister. Her husband pleaded with her to go home and take care of them, but she

Julianna Parker Monroe accompanied her husband into the military during the Civil War. This photograph of her in uniform, an albumen print, was taken around 1861. For albumen prints, which were extremely popular during the Civil War, albumen (a substance in egg whites) was used to bind the photographic chemicals to the paper.

insisted on staying in the army. "I was frightened half to death," she admitted later, "but I was so anxious to be with my husband that I resolved to see the thing through if it killed me."

Although her husband was hospitalized in October 1862, Martha stayed with the unit until her discharge in August 1864. Life as a soldier presented many new opportunities for her, and one of them turned out to be voting. In 1864, still in her disguise as Jim Smith, she cast a ballot for Abraham Lincoln to continue as president—the first and last vote of her life, since women could not legally vote until 1919.

Right before the war, two friends from Long Island, New York, Fanny Wilson and Nellie Graves, were visiting Fanny's relatives in Lafayette, Indiana. Both had left lovers behind and missed them greatly. While the young women were in Indiana, they learned that their sweethearts were planning to enlist in a new regiment that was being formed in New Jersey, the 24th New Jersey Infantry. Fanny and Nellie formulated a bold plan so they could be near these men; they returned home, went to the recruitment officer, and enlisted in the 24th New Jersey Infantry. But they did not tell the men what they intended to do.

During the war, the 24th fought at Chancellorsville, Virginia, and Wilson's young man died there. Both women fell ill after the battle and ended up in the army hospital in Cairo, Illinois. When their true identities became known, both were discharged from the army. No record exists of what happened to Nellie Graves, but Fanny Wilson, actually enlisted again, this time in the 3rd Illinois Cavalry, either to avenge the death of her beloved or because she enjoyed being a soldier.

Some women served with their brothers. A Tennessee woman from a poor mountain family with the splendid name of Melverina Elverina Peppercorn joined the Confederate army disguised as a man in order to be with her twin brother, Alexander the Great, called Lexy. When Lexy was shot in the leg and sent to the hospital, she left the army and accompanied him as his nurse.

The only woman known to have borne arms for both the Union and the Confederacy, Malinda Pritchard Blalock, served with her husband, Keith. When the war began, even though the Blalocks lived in North Carolina, a Confederate state, they supported Lincoln and the Union. Consequently, Keith and Malinda, an excellent hunter who could shoot a gun better than most men, provided food and shelter for Confederate deserters who passed their mountain cabin.

Malinda and Keith Blalock's cabin near Linville Falls, North Carolina, from a sketch by Shepherd Drugger in *War Trails of the Blue Ridge.*

Finally, when Keith was forced by recruiters to enter the Confederate army, Malinda—calling herself Sam Blalock, Keith's brother—signed up in the 26th North Carolina Infantry as well. A writer later said of Malinda, "She would have marched into the very jaws of death itself in her devotion to that which she held dear—Keith." Both Malinda and Keith hoped to get to the battlefront and at the first possible opportunity switch sides and join the Union army.

Because Sam excelled in cooking, the 26th selected her to take charge of it as the unit's "mess wife," although none of her fellow soldiers guessed how ironic the title actually was. Sam also spent long hours building fortifications. After several months of "miserable time in the Rebel army," she was wounded in a skirmish and taken to a surgeon for treatment. When the doctor discovered Malinda's true identity, Keith begged him to protect her secret for a few days. Then, in a desperate move, Keith rolled around naked in poison oak until his skin was swollen and covered with a red rash. Keith received a medical discharge; Malinda admitted to being his wife and was also released.

Later, because Keith recovered physically, he was labeled a "shirker and deserter" from the Confederate army. At this point, the couple headed to east Tennessee, so that they could join the Union forces now occupying the region. Enlisting in the 10th Michigan Cavalry, Keith became a recruiting officer and scout. He selected Sam as his aide-de-camp, and both put on Union uniforms. Soldiers in the 10th Michigan were flamboyant in their choice of uniforms, looking as much like

**Malinda Blalock, holding a picture of herself as Sam Blalock,
photographed after the Civil War.**

Russian Cossacks as they did like Union soldiers. Sam wore a sky blue greatcoat with a cape that she could pull over her head in rain or snow.

No one in the unit objected to the five-foot-four, 110-pound woman serving with her husband because of the respect that both Malinda and Keith engendered. Even so, Malinda continued to maintain her disguise as she guided Union soldiers and Rebel deserters through the North Carolina mountains. She carried a Colt revolver and a Spencer repeating rifle, one of the new Union guns far superior to anything she had ever used at home or as a Confederate soldier.

In September 1863, Malinda discovered that she was pregnant. She traveled to Knoxville, Tennessee, and later gave birth to a boy. During her absence, the 10th Michigan took part in a brief but bloody engagement at Warm Springs, Virginia. Keith later told people, "Malinda was sorry she missed the fight." Two weeks after the birth of their son, Malinda left the baby with relatives and returned to fight alongside Keith until the end of the war.

As the conflict continued and became less popular, fewer men enlisted. Consequently, each new recruit received a monetary reward, called a bounty. This financial incentive, along with the steady pay of a soldier, enticed some working-class and poor women to join the military. A working woman in civilian life could earn approximately $8 a month; hence, army wages—$13 a month early in the war and $16 later— seemed high to many laborers.

Sarah Rosetta Wakeman lived on a farm in New York

State. As her family's debts increased, she left home to find paying work. Since so few opportunities were open to her as a woman, she donned men's clothing and found employment on a river barge along a canal in Utica, New York.

During the canal trip, Rosetta met soldiers from the 153rd New York Infantry and decided to join them. As Lyons Wakeman, she enlisted in the regiment and received a bounty of $152, almost as much as she would have earned in a year as a laborer. She was very happy about her army pay and sent money to her family. "I am as independent as a hog on the ice," she wrote in a letter home.

A woman who took on the role of a man gained freedom she would never have had as a woman. Born and raised in Belfast, Ireland, Jennie Hodgers worked on a farm as a sheepherder and found that wearing boy's clothing made her life easier. Eager to emigrate to America, she stowed away on a ship dressed as a man; she remained in disguise as she eventually made her way to Belvidere, Illinois.

On August 3, 1862, she assumed the name of Albert D. J. Cashier and enlisted in the 95th Illinois Volunteer Infantry. She later reported, "Lots of boys enlisted under the wrong name. So did I. The country needed men, and I wanted excitement." She was a mere five feet tall, the shortest soldier in the unit. Although she did not receive any wounds or injuries during her long and difficult three-year term, Private Cashier was captured by Confederate troops. While being held prisoner, she seized the guard's rifle, knocked him down, and escaped to Union lines.

**Civil War photograph of Jennie Hodgers in uniform as
Albert D. J. Cashier, with an unknown army comrade.**

Some women enlisted simply for adventure and excitement. Although many of the facts that Loreta Janeta Velazquez reported in her memoir, *The Woman in Battle,* cannot be verified, some of the details appear to be accurate. She was born in Havana, Cuba, and came to the United States around 1849. She attended school in New Orleans and harbored a desire, formed in her childhood, to become a second Joan of Arc, the legendary French military leader of the 1400s. Swept up in the first wave of excitement about the war, she had a tailor prepare the appropriate uniform for her, and she joined the Confederate forces as Lieutenant Harry T. Buford.

As the war continued, some women became soldiers because of their desire to avenge a death. A few days after her fiancé was killed in a raid, Charlotte Hope, of Fairfax County, Virginia, became a member of the 1st Virginia Cavalry under the alias Charlie Hopper. She wanted to shoot twenty-one Yankees, one for every year of her beloved's life. But she refused to enter the ranks officially, because she would not take any pay for her efforts.

The women who fought as soldiers in the Civil War were extremely independent and individualistic. Each had unique reasons for wanting to take part in the conflict. But all shared an extraordinary degree of conviction and purpose. Consequently, they flouted convention and put on the uniform of a soldier.

High-fashion dresses for women, as shown in a wood engraving from
Frank Leslie's Illustrated Newspaper, March 1861. These particular dresses
were worn to Abraham Lincoln's inauguration ball.

3

"Don the breeches"

Enlisting in the Military

★ ★

*W*e know that some women were eager to fight in the Civil War, because they said so in their diaries. Sarah Morgan Dawson of Louisiana wrote: "Oh! If only I were a man! Then I could don the breeches and slay them with a will!" But to change sex required more than just desire; determination and action were also needed. One day Sarah stepped into a man's suit. She was "ashamed to let even my canary see me. . . . I have heard so many girls boast of having worn men's clothes; I wonder where they get the courage."

Unlike Sarah, some women found that courage. To join the military, a woman would first need to dress in entirely different clothes. In the 1860s women usually wore long dresses that reached the floor and—when they could afford them—hoop skirts, made of rings of steel wire and embellished with layers of fabric, lace, and ribbons. These enormous, rigid constructions sometimes caught on fire, because a woman could not control where the hem of her dress swept. Obviously, such an outfit would be ridiculous on the battlefield. A woman would also need to discard the corsets that kept her waist small and restricted her breathing. Then she needed to sew for herself or borrow and, probably for the first time, dress in the pants, called trousers or breeches, put on in those days only by men.

Normally, women wore their hair long, often arranged in elaborate constructions with braids, so a woman wanting to be a soldier would have to crop her hair quite short. If someone wore pants and had short hair, everyone assumed the person was a man. As one soldier wrote after a colleague's true identity was revealed, "A single glance at her in her proper character leads me to wonder how I ever could have mistaken her for a man . . . except that no one thought of finding a woman in a soldier's dress."

For a woman who wanted to fight, the next step—enlisting—generally proved a bit easier than assuming a male appearance. To begin the process, the would-be soldier had to find the nearest recruiter, regiment, or army camp, and present herself in disguise. Often she needed only to travel to the nearest town. During the Civil War, soldiers usually enlisted as members of voluntary units, created by local communities in each state. A town might form one or two companies, 100 people each; ten companies could be placed together to form a regiment of 1,000; forty companies made up a brigade.

Each recruit would be asked by a local official for his name, occupation, height, and age. At this time in history, no one possessed a birth certificate, Social Security number, photo ID, passport, or driver's license. In fact, no one carried any personal identification. Since soldiers had to be eighteen years old to enlist, many young boys lied about their age. A sixteen-year-old boy might take a piece of paper, write "18" on it, and place the paper in his shoe. When asked how old he was, he could say, honestly, "I am over eighteen." Usually the recruiter checked to make sure that the soldier appeared tall enough to fight, around five feet in height.

Then a local doctor or surgeon

A *carte de visite* of one of the many unnamed boy soldiers who fought in the Civil War, taken during the war by the Morris Gallery of Nashville, Tennessee. *Cartes de visite* ("visiting cards") were small albumen photographs, the size of calling cards, extremely popular in the 1860s. The prints were mounted on 2½-by-4-inch cardboard stock and fit into standard photograph albums.

would examine the candidates often in a superficial way. He might look first at the person's teeth, since a soldier needed teeth to rip open gunpowder cartridges. If a soldier had at least one upper tooth and one lower tooth that met, he could accomplish this task. Of course, teeth didn't reveal gender.

When Charles Baker of Massachusetts joined the army, a surgeon merely looked at him, felt his collarbones, and asked, "You have pretty good health, don't you?" When Sarah Emma Edmonds signed up as Franklin Thompson, all the examiner did was shake her hand and ask what sort of living that hand had earned. Doctors usually glanced at fingers and feet and rarely asked the recruit to remove clothing. One Union doctor had a reputation for being able to inspect ninety individuals each hour. At least 25 percent of the volunteers admitted into the Union army later proved physically unfit for duty—because the exams had been so cursory. Many women were able to slip into the ranks through the less-than-rigorous screening process.

In a few cases, men deliberately helped women into the military. A young Pennsylvania newlywed, Hattie Martin, wanted to serve with her husband in the ranks. She revealed this piece of information to the examiner, who accepted her for the army anyway. In the case of Harriet Merrill of the 59th New York, the captain of the regiment knew her identity and still allowed her to join.

However, not all women who tried to enlist succeeded. Union recruiters rejected a woman we know only as Miss Martin from Cincinnati five different times. Four times they refused to accept her because she was too short. At her fifth attempt, the doctor asked her to remove her clothes. Understandably, she didn't agree to this and hence was turned away again. Her failure to become a soldier bothered Miss Martin greatly because she knew many other girls who had slipped easily into the troops.

Some enterprising women skipped the enlistment process completely by joining a unit right before battle. To do this, a woman would need to find a uniform on her own, because soldiers usually were presented with the uniform of their particular regiment when they enlisted. Mary Galloway stole a uniform from her father, caught up with the Union army shortly before the Battle of Antietam, and attached herself to a group of soldiers without any exam or questions.

In her book, *The Woman in Battle,* Loreta Janeta Velazquez provided the most detailed account on record of how a woman might prepare to disguise herself as a man.

Loreta tried to convince her husband, William, who was joining the Confederate army, that she should go with him. However, he opposed her coming into the ranks, saying she would witness events impossible for such a "delicately nurtured and refined woman" to imagine. To give her insight into some of the conversation and behavior that he thought would upset her, he allowed her to dress up as a man and accompany him to a barroom, a place strictly off limits to women. However, his plan did not succeed. Although Loreta was afraid she might be recognized, she stayed and talked to men she actually knew, and she felt that she pulled off her

Loreta Janeta Velazquez in a barroom, testing out her male disguise.
Engraving by an unknown artist from *The Woman in Battle*.

act quite well. She even tried smoking a cigar, only to find that it made her dizzy.

When Loreta's husband set out for Richmond, Virginia, he believed that she had been cured of her insane desire to join the army. As soon as he left, though, she began plotting in earnest. Wearing his clothes, she went to a tailor and ordered two Confederate uniforms. Although the man had to measure her, he assumed that she was simply a young boy intent on fighting. Then she made some alterations to these uniforms. From another tailor she acquired a half dozen fine wire-net shields, which she arranged to conceal her shape. Over these she wore an undershirt of silk, held in place by straps. This top resembled the shoulder braces worn by men at the time. Around the waist of each undershirt she placed a band that made her waist appear to be larger than it was.

Then she had a friend cut her long and luxuriant hair, the one sacrifice that made her cringe. Next she went to the barber for a professional haircut, stained her face so that it looked tan, and added a false mustache to complete her ensemble. Thus prepared to pass as a man, she started off to the battlefront "with as stout a heart as ever beat in the breast of a soldier."

Once a woman had made it through the enlistment process, her real work began. A woman who wanted to remain a soldier had to look like a man and then act like a man at all times. She couldn't let her guard down for even a moment.

Fortunately for women trying to masquerade as men, Civil War soldiers changed clothes infrequently, and marched and slept in the same outfit. These ill-fitting uniforms concealed rather than revealed shapes. Although uniforms later became standardized, in the early years of the war, the armies permitted a great deal of diversity in attire. Uniforms often fell apart or were ruined in combat. It wasn't unusual to see soldiers wearing an odd assortment of garments. If need be, a woman could adjust her clothing to provide further concealment for herself. One of the members of the 6th

An engraving of Loreta Janeta Velazquez, signed **REA PHILA,** from *The Woman in Battle.*

New York Heavy Artillery explained how a woman in his regiment had maintained her disguise for close to three years: "We never undress to go to bed. . . . We go to bed with boots, overcoat and all on."

A woman in the ranks had to be extremely careful to maintain a male personality in everything she did. She needed to make sure that her voice stayed in the low male registers. She had to be observant to mimic the way men performed tasks. If a woman failed to watch her small actions, she frequently made mistakes. Even the way a

Loreta Janeta Velazquez in disguise as Lieutenant Harry T. Buford. Engraving signed REA from *The Woman in Battle.*

soldier picked up a leg to examine a shoe or boot could reveal identity. Sarah Collins of Wisconsin aroused suspicion because of the way she put on her shoes and stockings; Lizzie Cook of Iowa gave herself away by displaying refined table manners. When one of the officers of the 95th Illinois threw apples to six soldiers, four of them grabbed the fruit like men; the other two reached for nonexistent aprons to catch them in. These two women found themselves quietly removed from the unit.

Many beardless boys had entered the ranks, so a woman

Frances Clayton in a dress. Civil War photograph by Samuel Masbury.

did not have to pretend to shave. However, she might have to adopt other behavior that was considered manly—drinking alcohol, chewing tobacco, and gambling.

A member of the Minnesota State Militia Cavalry and the 2nd Minnesota Battery, Frances Louise Clayton (known also

Frances Clayton in uniform. Civil War photograph by Samuel Masbury.

as Clatin, Clalin, and Clailin) learned to do a variety of things associated with male behavior. She mastered spitting and chewing tobacco and then added smoking and drinking alcohol to her repertoire. She became extremely fond of cigars and also learned to play poker.

Confederate soldier Melverina Peppercorn could spit tobacco ten feet. She prided herself on her strength and her ability to shoot a gun as accurately as her twin brother, Lexy. Like many of the women in the war, Melverina was accustomed to the hard labor necessary for working on a farm, so she found the life of a soldier familiar in its daily routines. Women on farms and on the frontier often used rifles; many worked with horses. They had more experience with the basic demands of military life than their urban counterparts would today.

All in the army suffered from a lack of privacy that was especially challenging to women, who needed to find secluded areas for going to the bathroom. Generally, no one noticed if a shy soldier slipped away for private time or to take a bath in a river; however, no one bathed often. While marching from place to place, women probably drank little water, because they would have scant time for privacy. Hiding menstruation provided another problem. However, bloody cloths could always be disposed of—they might have been used to cover wounds. Also, because of weight loss, poor nutrition, extreme exercise, and skimpy diet, many women became lean and athletic while in the army and simply stopped menstruating.

Over time, a woman could settle into her new persona. But she always had to be on the alert. She needed to protect her secret. The average Civil War soldier did extraordinary things. But the women who fought accomplished everything that their male comrades did—while in a disguise and maintaining a continuous masquerade.

**Soldiers entertaining themselves in camp, watching roosters fighting.
Photograph by David Knox, Petersburg, Virginia, 1864.**

"A Skirmish drill is the prettiest drill"

A Soldier's Life

★ ★

A Civil War battle was very different from anything we see in news reports today. Tanks, planes, helicopters, trucks, jeeps, and long-range missiles hadn't been invented. The weapons used—rifles, cannons, and bayonets—are primitive to our modern eye. The infantry went into battle on foot. Each side shot at the other and tried to advance. Eventually, soldiers pulled out their bayonets and fought on the battlefield in hand-to-hand combat. When the battle ended, the survivors returned to camp and slept; the next day they began the ritual again. To our modern sensibility, 1860s warfare seems almost like a dance or a game with an elaborate set of rules.

Civil War soldiers did not arrive in the army with an understanding of those rules. The enlisted troops came untrained and unprepared for war. New recruits were almost comical in their attempts to simulate battlefield maneuvers. Infantrymen ran into one another while practicing with the bayonet. Cavalrymen scared their own horses while charging. Artillery units misfired their cannons. All soldiers—both men and women—had a lot to learn in order to be competent.

Before military units could fight, soldiers needed to be organized and trained. They generally received basic instruction on firing their new rifles, which varied from unit to unit and changed throughout the war. Then they might get more advanced training in using their equipment and in battle strategy. Some regiments focused on target practice. One Union officer set up a replica of Jefferson Davis, president of the Confederacy, for his men to shoot at. Some commanders conducted exercises, skirmish drills or mock battles, in which various groups—infantry, artillery, and cavalry—worked together on battle maneuvers. They used blank ammunition and simulated battle yells. Such maneuvers acclimated soldiers and horses to the smell of gunpowder and the deafening roar of the battlefield.

While not drilling, soldiers engaged in a variety of activities—digging fortifications, cleaning equipment, keeping watch. They might write letters to family and friends at home, whittle objects out of wood, keep a diary, or read. They also gambled, played cards, and bet on horse races—or anything else. They fitted tiny boats with paper sails and raced them for money. Even vermin—the louse, an insect that infested clothes—could be a source of entertainment. On a piece of canvas or a small dish, they would place two lice, then bet on which would leave the object first. Often camp life seemed so boring, it made recruits long for battle.

The letters and diaries kept by those who served are among the best sources of information we have about the day-to-day lives of Civil War soldiers. Few such records exist for the women soldiers, however, because this kind of record keeping or correspondence would have been risky. Only if her family wrote to her under her assumed—male—name would a woman have been able to receive mail. Since letters were sometimes read by military personnel, correspondents had to be very careful about what they revealed.

Only one set of Civil War letters written by a woman has been discovered, found in an attic trunk of one of her descendants. Sarah Rosetta Wakeman, at the age of nineteen, joined the 153rd New York Infantry as Lyons Wakeman on August 30, 1862. The five-foot-tall, brown-haired, blue-eyed soldier marched with the rest of her unit to Alexandria, Virginia, to help guard the capital, Washington, D.C., across the river.

From Rosetta's letters we get a sense of her adjustment to military life. "We all have a tin plate and a tin cup, and a knife and Fork, one spoon," she wrote. "We have to use the floor for a table." Evidently, even with the floor as a table, Rosetta ate better in the army than she ever had before. She

Civil War photograph of Sarah Rosetta Wakeman dressed in uniform as Lyons Wakeman.

told her family that she was getting fat as a hog, "the fattest fellow you will ever see."

Military life made Rosetta a happy woman. She enjoyed herself "better this summer than I ever did before in the world. I have good Clothing and enough to eat and nothing to do, only to handle my gun." She learned to keep her gun polished so highly that she could see her face in the barrel. Usually, she stood guard one day and drilled the next. "I like to drill first rate. . . . We load and fire our guns on drill. We fire blank cartridge. . . . I think a Skirmish drill is the prettiest drill that ever was a drill. I have got So that I can drill just as well as any man there is in my regiment."

In 1863, Lyons served as a guard at Carroll Prison, a military prison located in Washington, D.C. In one letter, she mentioned that three women had been confined there, one a major in the Union army. Although under attack, the major had ridden her horse into battle and given orders to her men.

This guard report for Carroll Prison in Washington, D.C., includes Lyons Wakeman's name.

But she had been put in prison because her sex had been discovered and hence she had violated the "regulations of war." The other two women prisoners, Belle Boyd and Ida P., had served as spies for the Confederacy.

From her letters we know that Rosetta sent a lot of money home ("I will send all the money I Can spare") and made friends with other soldiers ("I find just as good friends among Strangers as I do at home"). In fact, by the end of 1863, Rosetta was so pleased with army life that she contemplated joining the army for five years in another unit, in order to get $800 in bounty money then being promised to soldiers.

Even though Rosetta enjoyed being in the military, she must have experienced the typical hardships of Civil War soldiers. Their lives consisted of periods of tedium punctuated

Sketch of a typical battle scene; this Civil War drawing by Alfred R. Waud depicts a charge of the 6th Michigan Cavalry.

by periods of terror. When they received orders to proceed to the next battlefield, they first had to collect all their belongings and place them in a knapsack, which generally weighed between forty and fifty pounds when packed. Each soldier would carry a cartridge box, bayonet and scabbard, cap box, woolen blanket, canteen, underclothes, toothbrush, razor, soap, letters, mending kit, metal plate, knife, fork, spoon, and cup, and sometimes an overcoat. On long marches soldiers frequently threw out various items to lighten the load as they traveled across the countryside.

Marching in long lines, sometimes at night, the soldiers arrived at the battlefield on foot. Sarah Emma Edmonds observed:

> Three divisions moved forward, presenting a magnificent spectacle, as column after column wound its way over the green hills and through the hazy valleys, with the soft moonlight falling on the long lines of shining steel. Not a drum or bugle was heard during the march.

Soldiers called going into battle "seeing the elephant"—a contemporary expression connoting an awesome and exciting experience. A battle might begin with a short impromptu speech from the unit commander—"We are about to engage the enemy. Do your duty."—or simply a few words, such as "Aim low." A few minutes of silence, awful, lonely silence, prevailed before each encounter. Then, to intimidate the enemy, the troops on both sides entered battle with a furious cry: The Union screamed, "Huzza, huzza!"; the Confederacy's Rebel yell, high pitched, wild, has never been adequately described but terrorized Union troops.

The sounds of battle often proved deafening. A continual thundering noise emerged from cannons and guns, along with the cries of men screaming and bullets whistling all around. According to Loreta Janeta Velazquez,

> The sharp rattling of the musketry, the roar of the artillery, and the yelling of soldiers developed into an incessant tumult; while along the entire line, for miles, arose clouds of yellow dust and blue smoke, as the desperateness of the conflict increased.

At night the troops set up camp; the dead were buried and the wounded treated. Sometimes the two sides set aside hostilities and exchanged items in short supply. Along the Rappahannock River in Virginia, soldiers constructed small toy boats. One would be loaded with coffee and sent across the river from the Union camp to the Confederates; then a soldier unloaded the coffee, stocked the boat with tobacco, and sent it back. The next day the ritual of warfare resumed, and these same soldiers might face each other in hand-to-hand combat.

Many of those who enlisted found the realities of life as a soldier far more horrible than they had ever imagined. One

Loreta Janeta Velazquez, "Making a Charge."
Engraving by an unknown artist from *The Woman in Battle*.

man sarcastically described the glories of being a soldier in a letter to his wife: "Laying around in dirt and mud, living on hard tack, facing death in bullets and shells, eat[en] up by wood-ticks and body-lice." In the midst of fighting, participants experienced "battle frenzy," a high-adrenaline state that enabled them to fight the enemy. However, as they thought about the events afterward, the fighting often seemed much more dangerous and horrifying in memory than it had at the time.

Many soldiers found themselves ill prepared psychologically for the nightmare of battle. One said bluntly, "I have seen enough of the glory of war. . . . I am sick of seeing dead men and men's limbs torn from their bodies." Another soldier wrote, "The Twenty-fourth Ohio Volunteer Infantry had seen the elephant several times, and did not care about seeing him again unless necessary."

After their initial experience, why did soldiers keep going back again into conflict? Not all of them did. In 1863 an average of two hundred soldiers deserted from the Union or Confederate army every day. A woman soldier who wanted to leave the army did not have the same worries as a male deserter—which might include the mockery and disdain of friends and family or even a firing squad. She could simply walk away. If a woman soldier revealed her sex to an officer, he would discharge her from the army. Malinda Blalock could leave the Confederate army easily by revealing her real identity. Her husband, Keith, however, had to roll around in poison oak—a much more dangerous undertaking—to obtain his discharge.

A woman could take part in a battle, decide soldiering was not to her liking, and head for home. This may well have happened, unnoticed, hundreds of times in the war. We know about only the women who continued to fight; they lived with the horrors of conflict and chose to "see the elephant" again and again. Like the other soldiers of the Civil War, these women became part of something greater than themselves. They may have been motivated by a spirit of revenge; many of their loved ones and colleagues from their own military unit had been killed. They may have wanted to keep faith with their comrades, not wanting to let down the soldiers they had come to know. They may have held a cause—either Union or Confederate—dearer than they did their own personal safety.

These women went back into battle even though it would have been much easier to return home.

**Dead Confederate soldiers along Hagerstown Pike at Antietam.
One of a group of photographs taken by Alexander Gardner
in September 1862, right after the battle.**

5

"The whole landscape for an instant turned slightly red"

Women at Antietam

★ ★

Although all the Civil War battles have been recounted many times, only a few writers have ever thought to include the role of women, as well as men, in these descriptions. Since we now know more about the women soldiers who were fighting in the war, a more complete picture of each battle can be re-created if we also view their actions.

On September 17, 1862, at least eight women—seven for the Union, one for the Confederacy—participated in the Battle of Antietam in Maryland, a Union state. On the bloodiest day in American history, between 6,300 and 6,500 soldiers died and 13,000 were wounded. That single day

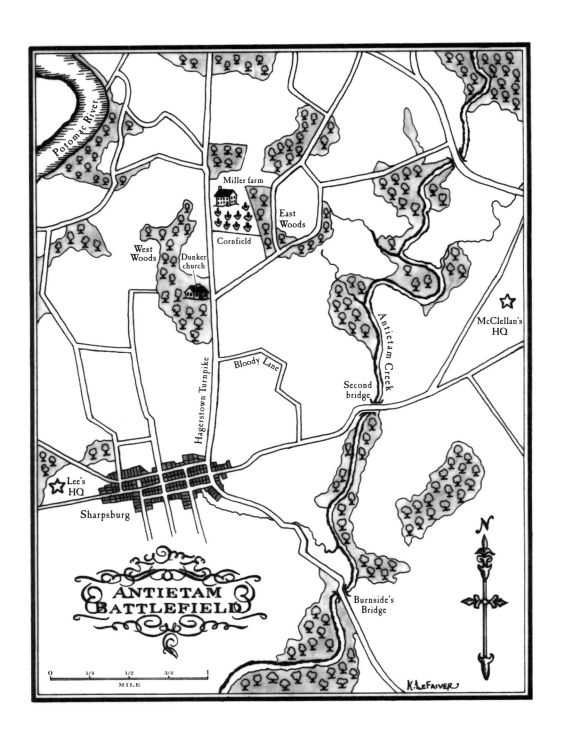

Potomac River

Miller farm

East
Woods

West
Woods

Dunker
church

Cornfield

McClellan's
HQ

Antietam Creek

Bloody Lane

Hagerstown Turnpike

Second
bridge

Lee's
HQ

Sharpsburg

ANTIETAM
BATTLEFIELD

Burnside's
Bridge

N

0   1/4   1/2   3/4   1
MILE

K. LeFaiver

claimed the lives of more Americans than all the other wars fought until then on North American soil, including the War of 1812, the Mexican-American War, the French and Indian Wars, and the American Revolution.

The battle took place in three distinct areas, near three bridges over Antietam Creek. By September 16, General Robert E. Lee's Confederate troops were stretched out for three miles along the meandering waterway. General George McClellan, head of the Union army, had a simple plan; he proposed to drive the Confederates into the creek and continue to pursue them until they left Maryland. Certainly, the day did not evolve the way either general thought it might.

The battle began near the first bridge. In the early morning, Union troops under General Joseph Hooker charged into a cornfield by the Miller farm, a site known for the rest of history simply as "the Cornfield." Here, Hooker encountered the legendary General Stonewall Jackson, who had a genius for outwitting the Union. At times each side gained ground, only to be pushed back again. The Cornfield changed hands five different times that morning. After a few hours, the slain soldiers lay in rows, precisely where they had stood in their ranks. One of the Confederate units, the 1st Texas, lost 82 percent of its members in the Cornfield. Among the dead lay an anonymous Confederate woman soldier, killed in the first phase of the battle.

The Iron Brigade engaged in the fiercest fighting in the Cornfield. Composed of the 2nd, 6th, and 7th Wisconsin and the 19th Indiana, the unit had been given its name at the

Peter Larsen in Iron Brigade uniform; ferrotype, 1864. Rebecca Peterman would have worn a similar outfit at Antietam. The photographic plates used in ferrotypes (later called tintypes) were made of iron.

Battle of South Mountain, which had occurred in the same area a few days earlier. As General McClellan watched his troops progress against stiff resistance up the gorge at South Mountain, he declared, "That brigade must be made of iron." Members of the Iron Brigade wore black felt hats adorned with brass, called Hardee hats. The 7th Wisconsin included in their ranks a woman soldier, Rebecca Peterman. She knew at least two other women from her Wisconsin county who fought in the war—so this brave Iron Brigade, with its distinctive hats, sported both male and female members.

Rebecca, sometimes called Georgianna, Peterman was from Ellenboro, Wisconsin, and had enlisted at the age of sixteen. Always an adventurous soul, she felt that "plain country life was not enough for her ambition." She wanted to experience war and be near her stepbrother and a male cousin, who encouraged her to join their regiment.

Even though her stepbrother died, Rebecca stayed with the regiment for two more years. Very small, with delicate hands, she had the walk and carriage of a boy. Outside of her relatives, no one knew her gender. In her first year, she spent some time as a drummer and then as a scout who "did good service with the musket." One soldier said that she was "one of the most gallant soldiers he ever saw." Although almost half of the Iron Brigade was killed or wounded in the Cornfield, Rebecca survived to continue fighting in the war.

Frank A. Haskell, a member of the 6th Wisconsin, later wrote about the some of the military action that Rebecca witnessed that day. The Iron Brigade

> moved out to battle a little after sunrise and before we had moved a hundred yards toward the enemy their second shell—the first just passed over our heads—dropped and exploded in the 6th Wisconsin and killed or wounded thirteen men and officers. . . . We moved on to battle and soon the whole ground shook at the discharges of

artillery and infantry. . . . At night we were in occupation of almost all we had gained of ground. . . . The enemy's dead and wounded were nearly all in our lines. . . . The loss of the Brigade was in killed and wounded, 880—47.5 percent of the men engaged.

Across from the Cornfield, the Union and Confederate troops fought near a small white church—the meetinghouse of the Dunkers, a German-American Baptist sect—where the Confederates had set up their artillery. In this area sixteen-year-old Mary Galloway fought for the Union. Mary, a resident of Frederick, Maryland, had a sweetheart named Harry

Battle raging around the Dunker church at Antietam.

The Dunker church with dead soldiers. Photograph by Alexander Gardner, September 1862.

Barnard, a Union lieutenant in the 3rd Wisconsin. Since all the men in Mary's family, and Harry, were participating in the war, she decided to locate Harry. Mary's father, a disreputable gambler and swindler, had acquired a box full of Union uniforms. Mary put one on, caught up with the army shortly before Antietam, and attached herself, presumably without too many questions being asked, to General William F. (Baldy) Smith's 6th Corps.

With members of three other regiments, Mary headed for the fighting near the Dunker church. She managed to get across Hagerstown Pike, the road in front of the church, but then Rebels launched an artillery bombardment. A bullet struck her in the neck and traveled to the right side of her back. She fell into a ravine while the battle raged around her.

The Union moved to capture a wooded area near the Dunker church, known as the West Woods. But rather than securing an easy victory, the soldiers actually marched into an ambush. The Rebels popped up from behind bushes, trees,

Burnside's Bridge. Photograph by Alexander Gardner, September 1862.

fence lines, and outcroppings, and fired on the surprised Union troops. These units suffered devastating losses: for example, 334 men of the 15th Massachusetts died. Falling near Mary Galloway was a fellow soldier, Oliver Wendell Holmes, Jr., who had also been shot through the neck. He lived to recount this battle, and to become the chief justice of the Supreme Court.

Civil War photograph of Oliver Wendell Holmes, Jr., in his Union officer's uniform.

By nine A.M., some 12,000 Americans had been killed or wounded: one for every second of the battle. Five Union and four Confederate divisions were completely wiped out.

Military activity on the field now shifted to the second bridge. Near it, a half mile of farm road had been seriously eroded by wagons. Several Confederate units took up a position in this natural, although somewhat shallow, trench, and they beat back one Union attack after another. So many dead lined Bloody Lane, as it was later called, that soldiers could walk the length of the road, stepping on bodies, and never touch the ground. Eventually, the Union broke the Confederate stronghold and took the center of the field.

General McClellan had at least 10,000 fresh Union troops available close to the second bridge in General William B. Franklin's 6th Corps. Franklin desperately wanted to bring his units into the battle, but McClellan decided against it. A woman soldier from New Jersey stood with the 1st Brigade, waiting to fight. She remained inactive that day, along with the rest of Franklin's regiments.

Near the third bridge—later called Burnside's Bridge, after the Union commanding officer, Ambrose Burnside—the Union troops included the Kanawha Division, which had helped win West Virginia's independence from Virginia. Lieutenant Colonel Rutherford B. Hayes and Sergeant William McKinley, future presidents of the United States, served in the 23rd Ohio, part of the Kanawha.

Fighting alongside the 23rd Ohio that day was Catherine

**Burnside's troops storming the Rebel position across Burnside's Bridge.
Wood engraving by Edwin Forbes, 1862.**

**The charge of Burnside's 9th Corps against the Confederate Army.
Pencil drawing by Edwin Forbes, September 17, 1862.**

E. Davidson, a member of the 28th Ohio. Although Burnside had 13,000 soldiers on this part of the field and Lee fewer than 4,000, the Confederates held the high ground, a heavily wooded area above the creek. There two Georgia regiments fired with deadly accuracy on the Union troops attempting to cross the bridge. Catherine became one of the casualties, her arm badly wounded by shrapnel.

Finally, a Union regiment forded the creek a mile away, and Burnside got his line moving. The 9th New York—one of the colorful Zouave regiments who dressed like the French Algerian army in skullcaps, short coats, and baggy trousers—made the most progress against the Confederates. The intensity of the fighting increased; as Union soldier David Thompson later wrote, "In a second the air was full of the hiss of bullets and the hurtle of grape-shot. The mental

**One of the colorful Zouave units, the 114th Pennsylvania, Company H.
Photographed near Petersburg, Virginia, August 1864.**

strain was so great that I saw at the moment . . . the whole
landscape for an instant turned slightly red."

One of the Zouaves was Ida Remington of Rochester,
New York. She had fought her first battle at South Mountain
and then marched to Antietam. Since these New York units
were close-knit groups and the members knew one another
by locality and occupation, it was particularly difficult for a
woman to sustain a male identity. But as later newspapers

reported, Ida demonstrated that "'when a woman will, she will,' regardless of the consequences." Ida used her determination not only to blend into the unit but to survive one of the worst battles of the war.

Toward the end of the day, the fighting came to a standstill. As night fell, the battlefield was a place of horror, beyond imagination—a scene of utter devastation and ruin. A Union official wrote: "For four miles in length, and nearly half a mile in width, the ground is strewn with . . . hats, caps, clothing, canteens, knapsacks, shells and shot." Scattered around were "long mounds of earth, where, underneath, five thousand men, wrapped in their blankets, were laid side to side."

In the Cornfield, the burying party from the 10th Massachusetts Infantry discovered a woman among the Confederate dead. Mark Nickerson of the 10th wrote that news of her existence spread among the soldiers, who went "and gazed upon the upturned face, and tears glistened in many eyes as they turned away. . . . Nothing in my experience up to that time affected me as did that incident. I wanted to know her history and why she was there." They wrapped her in a soldier's blanket, placed her in a grave by herself, and made a marker "unknown woman CSA [Confederate States of America]."

Another woman, one who fought for the Union, received a special burial that day. That soldier was discovered by Sarah Emma Edmonds, who, in her disguise as Private Franklin Thompson, was providing medical aid for soldiers at

Dead Confederate soldiers of Stonewall Jackson's brigade by the fence on Hagerstown Pike. Photograph by Alexander Gardner, September 1862.

Antietam. As she worked, she was drawn to the pale, sweet face of a youthful soldier, severely wounded in the neck. The soldier, growing faint from loss of blood, turned clear, intelligent eyes on Edmonds and said simply, "I am dying." When the surgeon came by, he declared that nothing could be done and left Edmonds to administer brandy and water.

Then the soldier spoke again.

"I am not what I seem, but am a female. I enlisted from the purest motives, and have remained undiscovered and unsuspected. I have neither father, mother nor sister. My only brother was killed today. I closed his eyes about an hour before I was wounded. . . . I am a Christian, and have maintained the Christian character ever since I entered the army. I have performed the duties of a soldier faithfully, and am willing to die for the cause of truth and freedom. . . . I wish you to bury me with your own hands, that none may know after my death that I am other than my appearance indicates."

Edmonds sought out a chaplain and prayed; then she buried the soldier under the shadow of a mulberry tree—near the battlefield but apart from the others.

Some of the women wounded at Antietam lived to tell different, and happier, stories. Near Burnside's Bridge, Andrew Curtin, the governor of Pennsylvania, helped with rescue efforts as a civilian. He consoled Catherine E. Davidson, whose arm had been shattered, and put her in an ambulance. In appreciation for his aid, she gave him her ring.

Later, after a surgeon had amputated the arm and Davidson had been released from service, she called upon Governor Curtin at the Continental Hotel in Philadelphia, kissed him on the forehead, and thanked him for what he had done. The shocked governor had had no idea that the

"An interesting patient": Sarah Emma Edmonds cares for a dying
female soldier at Antietam. Wood engraving by R. O'Brien
from *Nurse and Spy in the Union Army,* 1864.

soldier who had given him a ring was a woman. He wanted
to return it to her, but she asked him to keep it: "The finger
that used to wear that ring will never wear it any more. The
hand is dead, but the soldier still lives."

Mary Galloway lay in the ravine on the other side of the
Dunker church for thirty-six hours. Then she was taken to a
shed behind one of the farmhouses, the building that served
as a hospital. Clara Barton, the nurse called "the angel of the
battlefield," had been there all day. While tending wounded
soldiers, Barton often came into harm's way, and by the end
of the day she wore clothing torn by bullets. Mary feared the

discovery of her identity and refused to let the male doctor near her. He summoned Barton, who succeeded in calming the patient. Without using anesthesia, the surgeon then removed the bullet in her upper back and turned the soldier over to Barton. Bearing her pain bravely, Mary revealed her secret and told about her search for her lover.

Soon afterward, Barton located Galloway's sweetheart, Harry Barnard, in a Fredericksburg, Virginia, hospital. Mary

A lone grave on Antietam, much like the one described by Sarah Emma Edmonds in *Nurse and Spy in the Union Army*. Photograph by Alexander Gardner, September 1862.

traveled there and stayed with the wounded Harry, whose arm had been amputated. Eventually, they married; they named their first child Clara Barton Barnard.

During the night of September 17, Lee withdrew his army from the battlefield and headed out of Maryland, back to Virginia. Although his army had not been destroyed by the battle, it had been badly hurt. There was one positive outcome from the bloodshed and carnage of Antietam. On September 22, five days after this Union victory, President Abraham Lincoln issued a proclamation warning the Confederate states that if they did not return to the Union by January 1, 1863, their slaves "shall be then, thenceforward, and forever free."

**President Abraham Lincoln and General George McClellan
in the general's tent after the Battle of Antietam.
Photograph by Alexander Gardner, September 1862.**

"I would rather have been shot dead"

Hospitals and Prisons

★ ★

For soldiers in the Civil War, the risk of illness was far more frightening than getting injured on the battlefield. In the days before antibiotics, twice as many soldiers succumbed to disease as died from wounds. For a woman soldier, both possibilities held another danger. Even if she recovered her health, being under a doctor's care would likely mean that her true identity would be revealed and she would be discharged from the army. Mary Scaberry of Columbus, Ohio, served in the 52nd Ohio as Charles Freeman. After the seventeen-year-old became ill and was admitted to a hospital in Louisville, Kentucky, the doctor diagnosed her ailment and also stated that she suffered from "sexual incompatibility"—meaning that she was the wrong sex to be in the army—and sent her home.

The true identity of the woman known as Private Frank Martin has never been discovered. She was born in 1845 in Pennsylvania. To enlist, she headed for Louisville, Kentucky, where she joined the 2nd Tennessee Cavalry. During the Battle of Stones River, Private Martin, severely wounded in the shoulder, arrived at the hospital. There the physician found out her secret, and a general ordered her removed from the regiment. Undeterred, Private Martin joined the 8th Michigan Infantry. A seasoned veteran, good soldier, experienced scout, and excellent horsewoman, she served as a regimental bugler and was eventually transferred to the 25th Michigan. This time, even after a soldier from her hometown recognized her, the regimental commander allowed her to stay; he must have decided that his need for a good soldier outweighed the fact that she was a woman.

Because Sarah Emma Edmonds wrote her own memoirs and applied for a federal pension for her army services, we know more about her than we do about most women soldiers, including how she responded to illness. Sarah joined the Union army right after President Lincoln called for volunteers in 1861, and as Private Franklin Thompson became part of the 2nd Michigan Infantry. The 2nd Michigan participated in most of the major battles of the Civil War, including First Bull Run, Fredericksburg, Antietam, and Second Bull Run. While in the infantry, Private Thompson not only fought but also became known as a skilled medical nurse,

**Portrait of Sarah Emma
Edmonds. Wood engraving
by R. O'Brien from** *Nurse
and Spy in the Union Army,*
1864.

someone who cared for patients but did not perform surgery.
Then Sarah applied to become an agent, or spy, gathering
information on the Confederate operations at Yorktown,
Virginia; she succeeded so well that General McClellan sent
her on ten other espionage missions.

Early in 1863, Private Thompson contracted a severe case
of malaria. She survived the first bout of chills and fever without seeking medical treatment. In March the 2nd Michigan
was transferred to Lebanon, Kentucky; Thompson stayed
with them, suffering severe fevers and becoming delirious.

A *carte de visite* **of Sarah Emma Edmonds in female attire.**

Although comrades repeatedly urged the soldier to go to the hospital, she knew that a hospital stay would reveal her true identity. Denied a leave of absence, she fled from the army and headed north to Oberlin, Ohio, where she spent weeks recovering. She didn't consider herself a deserter; on the contrary, she was taking steps to avoid being discovered and discharged from the military. "I would rather have been shot dead, than to have been known to be a woman and sent away from the army," she wrote. After recovering, she decided to

A *carte de visite* **of Sarah Emma Edmonds as Private Franklin Thompson.**

rejoin the army as a war nurse—under her real name—and she served until the end of the war.

At least six women remained undiscovered in the army until they gave birth to babies. Colonel Elijah H. C. Cavins, a Union officer with a sense of humor, wrote home that "a corporal was promoted to sergeant for gallant conduct at the battle of Fredericksburg—since which time the sergeant has become the mother of a child."

During and after battles, both the Union and the

Photograph of Andersonville Prison, Georgia, August 1864.

Confederacy rounded up enemy soldiers and made them prisoners of war. Although some were returned to their units as part of a prisoner exchange—in which the two sides swapped captured soldiers—some were sent to prison. Prisoners on both sides suffered from lack of food, over-crowded facilities, and inadequate sanitary conditions. If captured, a woman might be detained in prison along with others from her unit. Usually, if she revealed her true identity, she would be released and sent home. But some women chose to stay in disguise and remain with their comrades, enduring the terrible conditions of prison life.

Mary Ann, sometimes called Amy or Anna, Clarke of Iuka, Mississippi, enlisted in a Louisiana cavalry regiment at the age of thirty. After her husband's death in the war, she joined the 11th Tennessee. Wounded in battle, Clarke was captured by the Union and placed in a prison in Cairo, Illinois, along with two other women soldiers. Promising to resume her life as a civilian, Mary Ann returned to Mississippi, but once there she announced her intention to rejoin the army. Although no further record of her exists, it is believed that she did become a soldier again—that neither battle wounds nor prison deterred her.

Some women did their best to get out of prison without revealing their true identity. Frances Hook, a Union soldier under the alias Frank Miller, had enlisted at the age of fourteen with her brother in the 65th Illinois Home Guards. Since her brother was her only living relative, Frances wanted to stay with him. Later, when her term of service expired, she re-enlisted in the 90th Illinois. Taken prisoner by the Confederates in Alabama in 1863, Frank Miller attempted to escape and was shot in the thigh. After a medical exam, the Confederate authorities promptly got rid of her in the next prisoner exchange.

Imprisoned seven times, Mary Jane Green of the Confederacy holds the record for the greatest number of Civil War incarcerations for a woman. She was first captured in Braxton County, Virginia, and released when she promised to leave the army. Continuing as a Confederate soldier, Mary Jane fell into Union hands again. This pattern continued until the unlucky woman's seventh capture; then she remained in Old Capitol Prison in Washington, D.C., until the end of the war.

In 1864 the Confederacy set up a new prison in Georgia, a twenty-six-acre camp named Andersonville. It became the most overcrowded, unsanitary, and brutal facility of the war, sometimes holding as many as 30,000 prisoners. The death toll rose to close to 13,000. Many of the soldiers who were lucky enough to be released from Andersonville, "a filthy zoo not even fit for animals," later died from medical complications contracted there.

A large group of soldiers seen from the main gate of Andersonville. Wood engraving published in *Harper's Weekly,* 1866.

Andersonville housed at least three women. One of them, Janie Hunt, continued to disguise herself as a man so that she might remain with her husband, a prisoner there. Janie actually gave birth to a baby at Andersonville; then authorities permitted her to board at a farm near the prison.

Another of these prisoners, Florena Budwin, came from Philadelphia and had enlisted with her husband, Captain Budwin. In 1864, Florena and her husband were captured and taken to Andersonville, where he died. Still in disguise, Florena was transferred to a new prison at Florence, South Carolina, where she helped care for sick and wounded soldiers. When she herself became ill, a doctor discovered her secret. She died in prison and was buried in the National Cemetery in Florence, South Carolina.

Like their male comrades in arms, women soldiers prepared for battle, fought, and took the consequences of engaging an enemy. They became ill, were sent to hospitals, or were made prisoners of war. But many of them, with amazing resilience, did not seek dismissal even under these conditions. Whenever possible, they continued to masquerade as men.

A modern photograph of Private Lyons Wakeman's tombstone, Chalmette National Cemetery, New Orleans, Louisiana.

"Touched with fire"

After the War

★ ★

On April 9, 1865, General Robert E. Lee acknowledged the Union victory by surrendering to General Ulysses S. Grant at Appomattox Court House in Virginia. After this official ending of the Civil War, soldiers began to return home. Of the 3.5 million who fought, 620,000 died. Many female soldiers didn't come home; death put an end to their masquerade.

During one battle, Lieutenant Rutherford B. Hayes, future president of the United States, ordered the 5th West Virginia Cavalry to seek shelter. Everyone obeyed except a mounted cavalryman, who argued with him. Then an enemy bullet struck the soldier. Rushing to see if anything could be done, a doctor discovered that the dead private was a woman. She had enlisted in the army to avenge her father and brother, both killed by the enemy.

Sarah Rosetta Wakeman died in a New Orleans hospital, leaving behind a silver ring, which she had engraved with her name and 153RD N.Y. VOL. REGIMENT. She was buried in New Orleans.

For a few living women soldiers, the transition to civilian life proved hard, almost impossible. Unlike their male comrades, they received no hero's welcome upon returning home. Rebecca Peterman had served with honor in the Iron Brigade; discharged from the 7th Wisconsin, she headed to her home in Ellenboro, Wisconsin. While in Chicago, still in disguise, she was robbed of her papers and money. When Rebecca finally arrived home, the press began to hound her. For a period of time she became a fugitive, traveling from one small Wisconsin town to another, in the hope of avoiding her unwanted notoriety.

In August 1864, after serving in disguise and being wounded three times, Mary Ellen Wise of Indiana went to Washington, D.C., to demand pay for her service. Although her request was refused by the paymaster general (who believed that army regulations did not authorize payment to women soldiers passing as men), her case came to the attention of President Abraham Lincoln; he ordered that she be compensated immediately. A month later Mary Ellen married a fellow soldier, Sergeant Lloyd Forehand. Then, according to newspaper accounts, she started to follow her husband

1865 army discharge papers for Private Lyons Wakeman.

around with a pistol, threatening to take his life. She may have been suffering from what we now call post-traumatic shock, caused by fighting in the war, a condition that was not understood at the time.

Jennie Hodgers, also known as Private Albert D. J. Cashier of the 95th Illinois Infantry, served with her unit for three years and left on August 27, 1865. She chose an

Woman Soldier in 95th Ill.

ALBERT D. J. CASHIER
OF
COMPANY G, 95TH ILLINOIS REGIMENT

Photographed November, 1864

ALBERT D. J. CASHIER
OF
COMPANY G, 95TH ILLINOIS REGIMENT

Photographed July, 1913

Newspaper article showing Jennie Hodgers as
Albert D. J. Cashier in 1864 and in 1913.

unusual path after the war. Still disguised as a man, she settled in Saunemin, Illinois. For the next forty years, she worked as a janitor, a handyman, and the town lamplighter. In 1890 she applied for, and received, a pension. Fifteen people testified about Albert Cashier's military service; a physician signed a letter saying that Cashier was completely disabled.

But in 1911, when her leg was crushed, a doctor discovered her secret. First admitted to the Illinois Soldiers' and Sailors' Home, she developed a form of dementia as she aged and was eventually placed in a mental institution. Newspaper articles about her began to appear in 1914, and her old comrades in arms came to her defense. Veterans of the 95th visited her; all praised her abilities as a soldier. After she died, she received a full military funeral, with a flag draped over her coffin. Her tombstone read simply, ALBERT D. J. CASHIER, CO. G 95 ILL. INF.

Many of the returning male soldiers received special honors; occasionally females also got that recognition. African American Maria Lewis served for eighteen months in the 8th New York Cavalry. Designated a member of an honor guard, she presented seventeen captured Confederate flags to the War Department. Northern abolitionists, assisting freed slaves in Alexandria, Virginia, helped Lewis in the transition to civilian life and freedom.

Most female soldiers simply returned to their homes, resuming their traditional roles. Some did not even talk about their military service. Martha Parks Lindley was discharged in

Recent photograph of a modern tombstone for Jennie Hodgers, providing her military history, Sunny Slope Cemetery, Saunemin, Illinois.

August 1864, went home, and retrieved her children from her sister. Then the family moved to Cleveland, Ohio, and Lindley had two more children. Although they wouldn't talk to the press, Martha and her husband regaled their children with war stories. The children saved their mother's uniform and pistol and passed them down to the next generation.

When Elizabeth Finneran's husband, John, applied for his pension, several of his commanding officers mentioned the service of his wife, Elizabeth. When she died, a lengthy obituary presented her service record, and her achievement was also noted on her tombstone. In death she received the recognition that she had not sought in her lifetime; she was buried with full military honors.

While a new bride, Lucy Gauss had served as sharpshooter Private Bill Thompson for the 18th North Carolina, the unit to which her husband, Bryant, belonged. Wounded at the First Battle of Bull Run, Lucy continued to fight in the war until Bryant was killed. Then in an advanced stage of pregnancy, she obtained a permanent leave and took his body home for burial. Around 1866 this widowed mother remarried in Savannah, Georgia, and she eventually had six more children. She always lived by her motto: "Hold your head up and die hard."

In 1914, Lucy Gauss Kenney, as an old woman, revealed her Civil War service to her pastor. She had chosen to keep her role secret for over fifty years.

Some women returned home wanting to tell their stories. Frances Clayton was discharged in Louisville in 1863 and headed back to Minnesota.

Photograph of Lucy Gauss Kenney, alias Private Bill Thompson, around 1920 at her home in Georgia.

Later, she began to perform onstage, recounting her experiences in the war. As a woman soldier, she could depend on people's curiosity about her adventures to gather a crowd. A poster advertising her performance at the Institute Hall on February 25, 1865, indicates that she appeared in uniform. Clayton went through sword exercises, made general remarks, and offered her picture for sale.

Only two women are known to have recorded their military lives in memoirs. Sarah Emma Edmonds wrote *Nurse and Spy in the Union Army* while recuperating from malaria. Published in 1864, it quickly sold 175,000 copies, an astounding number for the time. Edmonds donated the proceeds to care for sick and wounded Union soldiers. Later, Edmonds took courses at Oberlin College, married, had three children, adopted two sons, and became a member of the Grand Army of the Republic, the organization of Union veterans of the Civil War. She applied for, and received, a military pension, and upon her death in 1898 she was buried with full military honors.

After the war Loreta Janeta Velazquez joined her brother, another Confederate veteran, on a tour of Europe. She returned to New Orleans in 1867. The *New Orleans Times Picayune* reported, "It is very difficult for us to recognize in the rather graceful . . . lady in black . . . the rather shabby looking Lieut. Bufort [*sic*] of Confederate times." Adopting several names and marrying many husbands, Velazquez became an agent for the Venezuelan Emigration Company, traveled to Venezuela and Cuba, and ended up in Texas. In

MRS. F. L. CLATIN,

FROM MINNESOTA, who enlisted and was with her husband, twenty-two months in the Western army, was in 18 skirmishes, and two hard fought battles, and can give a good account of herself as a cavalry soldier.

MRS. CLATIN IS NO IMPOSTOR. She has her papers with her, and can satisfy any one who doubts her story. She will give a history of her life up to the time of her enlistment.

She will then appear in disguise as she did when she enlisted. She will also appear in cavalry rig, and go through with the sword exercise.

Lastly, she will appear in her woman's attire, and make some remarks as to her present condition.

Go and see the Heroine of the West, the only woman that has suffered so much, and lived to tell her story. She was wounded three times, and is now a cripple.

Her picture will be for sale at the close of the lecture.

The entertainment will be interspersed with music.

MRS. CLATIN WILL LECTURE TO NIGHT, at *the*

Institute Hall

Feb 29

TICKETS 25 CENTS.
Children under 12 years of age 15 Cents.

Doors open at 6 1-2 to commence at 7 1-2 o'clock.

T. FAY, AGENT.

Feb. 1865.

A flyer advertising a performance by Frances Clayton, who told her story as the "Heroine of the West" wearing full military uniform.

1876, she published an account of her experience, *The Woman in Battle,* hoping that the revenue would support her. Velazquez claimed patriotism and a desire for adventure as her only reasons for service and made no excuses or apologies for her actions. Extremely controversial, the book was denounced by some Confederate officers, who believed the story a fabrication; but others, including General James Longstreet, vouched for her service.

During and after the war, many newspaper articles, memoirs, and books—such as Frank Moore's *Women of the War,*

Women visiting wounded soldiers, sewing and washing garments, and writing a letter for a soldier. Wood engraving from *Harper's Weekly,* September 1862.

published in 1866—contained information about the women who had dressed like men and fought for the North and South. But Victorian writers of the 1880s and 1890s found the idea of military action inconsistent with their image of a true woman—pious, pure, submissive, and domestic. The popular press seized on the role of women as nurses and spies in the war, but passed over the stories of those who had served as soldiers. By the twentieth century, women soldiers received scant mention, if any at all. Histories of the Civil War ignored these women, as did Ken Burns in his otherwise exemplary television documentary on the Civil War, produced in the 1990s.

Only in the past few years has a group of women historians attempted to set the record straight on the contributions of women soldiers. Because of the work of these writers, we now have a more accurate picture of the role of women in the Civil War. Several hundred women took their fate into their own hands and slipped into the military, joining their male comrades because they wanted to serve as soldiers. Oliver Wendell Holmes, Jr., chief justice of the United States, summed up the Civil War experience of his generation with these words: "In our youth our hearts were touched with fire." When we think about the bravery of those who fought in the Civil War, we can now honor the passionate women whose hearts were also touched with fire and who went to extraordinary lengths to serve as soldiers.

Civil War photograph of a Union camp, with troops in formation
and tents in the background.

AUTHOR'S NOTE

★ ★

This book began more than thirty years ago. Right after my grandmother died in 1975, I traveled to Marietta, Ohio, for her funeral and spent time with my parents going through my grandparents' home. Looking through an old photo album, I was mesmerized by a picture of three young boys in Civil War uniforms, unidentified members of the McKitrick family. That picture haunted me for another fifteen years, until I began researching my family history, trying to put names to those three winsome faces.

I searched libraries, walked Civil War battlefields, spent days in the National Archives with governmental records, and read Civil War regimental accounts. In doing this research, I became an armchair Civil War buff, picking up biographies and battle accounts in my spare time. I fell in love with my Union ancestors and the remarkable Confederate generals. Eventually, I considered myself knowledgeable; then, one day, someone recommended DeAnne Blanton and Lauren M. Cook's *They Fought Like Demons*, the most comprehensive book to date on women soldiers in the Civil War. Suddenly, I felt as if I knew nothing; I had never heard of—or even thought about—the women who fought in the war.

With my editor Dinah Stevenson's encouragement, I

embarked on a four-year journey, trying to understand these remarkable soldiers. I began my research by asking myself, "Why did they enlist?" and spent time talking to veterans of World War II and to psychologists in order to frame an answer. Ultimately, I had to ask, "Why did they stay?"

I began my research at the Manassas (Bull Run) National Battlefield, escorted by Anne McCracken and Sarah Hopwood of the Fairfax (Virginia) County Schools. The terrain remains unspoiled and serene, the work of many groups, including the Civil War Preservation Trust, to protect this hallowed ground. At Bull Run I traced the movements of Loreta Janeta Velazquez and Sarah Emma Edmonds, two women who were present at the battle and who wrote memoirs.

From that point on, researching women in the Civil War wasn't any different from researching my own Civil War ancestors. I read pension files, hunted for old newspaper articles, went through Civil War regimental accounts; I read novels like *The Killer Angels* and decades of *Civil War Times Illustrated*. I witnessed military reenactments and watched all the available videos and movies featuring these units. In the process I grew frustrated with how little we know about many of these women; some names appear only in one newspaper article or one military record. But I kept hoping that more material would surface.

After about a year of research, I traveled to the Civil War mecca, Gettysburg, to walk the battlefield early in the morning and late at night, to attend lectures, and to search

for snippets of information. Then I went to Antietam to follow the movements of the eight women known to have
fought there. The articles and books about Antietam that I
had consulted never described the experiences of the
women who participated. I wanted a soldier's-eye view for
each of them: to see where they stood, what they saw, and
where they lay wounded. Mary Galloway was especially
challenging. I knew she fell into a ravine and even believed
that I had located the spot—not far from where Oliver
Wendell Holmes, Jr., was shot. But according to official
records, Mary's unit stayed in reserve, a half mile away,
and I couldn't reconcile these facts. Fortunately, Stephen
Sears, in his great book on Antietam, *Landscape Turned Red*,
provided the needed clue.

I'm not descended from these women soldiers in reality;
but in spirit I grew to love them, understand them, and feel
kinship with them. I only hope, as an author, that I have
done justice to their stories.

**Civil War photograph of Kady Brownell in the uniform she wore
as a daughter of the regiment for the 1st Rhode Island Infantry.**

BIBLIOGRAPHY

★ ★

BOOKS

Blanton, DeAnne, and Lauren M. Cook. *They Fought Like Demons: Women Soldiers in the American Civil War.* Baton Rouge, La.: Louisiana State University Press, 2002.

Burgess, Lauren Cook, ed. *An Uncommon Soldier: The Civil War Letters of Sarah Rosetta Wakeman, Alias Private Lyons Wakeman, 153rd Regiment, New York State Volunteers.* Pasadena, Md.: The Minerva Center, 1994.

Catton, Bruce. *Reflections on the Civil War.* Edited by John Leekley. Edison, N.J.: Promontory Press, 1981.

Clinton, Catherine, and Christine Lunardini. *The Columbia Guide to American Women in the Nineteenth Century.* New York: Columbia University Press, 2000.

Dannett, Sylvia G. L. *She Rode with the Generals: The True and Incredible Story of Sarah Emma Seelye, Alias Franklin Thompson.* New York: Thomas Nelson, 1960.

Dawson, Sarah Morgan. *A Confederate Girl's Diary.* Boston: Houghton Mifflin, 1913.

de Pauw, Linda Grant. *Battle Cries and Lullabies: Women in War from Prehistory to the Present.* Norman, Okla.: University of Oklahoma Press, 1998.

Durrant, Lynda. *My Last Skirt: The Story of Jennie Hodgers, Union Soldier.* New York: Clarion Books, 2006.

Edmonds, Sarah Emma. *Memoirs of a Soldier, Nurse and Spy: A Woman's Adventures in the Union Army.* DeKalb, Ill.: Northern Illinois University Press, 1999. A modern edition of the book published in her lifetime as *Nurse and Spy in the Union Army.*

Eggleston, Larry G. *Women in the Civil War: Extraordinary Stories of Soldiers, Spies, Nurses, Doctors, Crusaders, and Others.* Jefferson, N.C.: McFarland & Company, 2003.

Harper, Judith E. *Women During the Civil War: An Encyclopedia.* New York: Routledge, 2004.

Hoar, Jay S. *The South's Last Boys in Gray: An Epic Prose Elegy.* Bowling Green, Ohio: Bowling Green State University Popular Press, 1986.

Leonard, Elizabeth D. *All the Daring of the Soldier: Women of the Civil War Armies.* New York: W. W. Norton, 1999.

McClellan, Elisabeth. *History of American Costume 1607–1870.* New York: Tudor, 1973.

McPherson, James M. *Crossroads of Freedom: Antietam.* New York: Oxford University Press, 2002.

Moore, Frank. *Women of the War: Their Heroism and Self-Sacrifice.* Hartford, Conn.: S. S. Scranton, 1866.

Oates, Stephen B. *A Woman of Valor: Clara Barton and the Civil War.* New York: Free Press, 1994.

Perry, James M. *Touched with Fire: Five Presidents and the Civil War Battles That Made Them.* Cambridge, Mass.: Public Affairs, 2003.

Sears, Stephen W. *Landscape Turned Red: The Battle of Antietam.* Boston: Houghton Mifflin, 1983.

Shaara, Michael. *The Killer Angels.* New York: McKay, 1974.

Stevens, Peter F. *Rebels in Blue: The Story of Keith and Malinda Blalock.* Dallas, Tex.: Taylor Publishing, 2000.

Taylor, Susie King. *A Black Woman's Civil War Memoirs.* New York: Marcus Wiener Publishing, 1988.

Velazquez, Loreta Janeta. *The Woman in Battle: The Civil War Narrative of Loreta Janeta Velazquez, Cuban Woman and Confederate Soldier.* Madison, Wis.: University of Wisconsin Press, 2003.

Welter, Barbara. *Dimity Convictions: The American Woman in the Nineteenth Century.* Athens, Ohio: Ohio University Press, 1976.

Wiley, Bell Irving. *The Life of Billy Yank: The Common Soldier of the Union.* Baton Rouge, La.: Louisiana State University, 1978.

———. *The Life of Johnny Reb: The Common Soldier of the Confederacy.* Baton Rouge, La.: Louisiana State University, 1978.

ARTICLES AND ARCHIVAL MATERIAL

American Antiquarian Society. Invitations & Notices. Box 1. Untitled flyer. Worcester, Mass.

"Another Female Soldier." *Fincher's Trades' Review,* August 22, 1863.

"Another Female Soldier." *St. Paul Pioneer,* February 19, 1865.

Clausius, Gerhard P. "The Little Soldier of the 95th: Albert D. J. Cashier." *Journal of the Illinois State Historical Society,* Vol. 51 (Winter 1958).

Davis, Rodney. "Private Albert Cashier, as Regarded by His/Her Comrades." *Journal of the Illinois State Historical Society,* Vol. 82 (Summer 1989).

"A Female Soldier." *Chicago Evening Journal,* February 13, 1865.

Haskell, Frank A. Letter. http://www.secondwi.com/fromthefront/7th%20wis/1982/7thoct62.htm

Herek, Raymond J. "A Woman in the Regimentals." *Civil War Times Illustrated,* January 22, 1984.

Hunter, Bethuel. "No Man Can Hinder Me." 2003. Beinecke Rare Book and Manuscript Library. New Haven, Conn.

National Archives Administration. Veteran's Administration. Pension application files. Finneran, John.

National Archives Administration. Veteran's Administration. Pension application files. Seelye, S. Emma [the former Sarah Edmonds].

"Remarkable Incident." *Princeton (Indiana) Clarion,* November 14, 1863.

"Romance of an Ohio Woman Who Fought by Her Husband's Side." *Cleveland Leader,* October 7, 1896.

"Women Soldiering as Men." *New York Sun,* February 10, 1901.

SOURCE NOTES

★ ★

Full information on the sources cited here can be found in the Bibliography, beginning on page 99.

Chapter One

PAGE

2   "at the prospect before me": Velazquez, p. 95.

4   "In gay spirits": Edmonds, p. 12.

5   Number of women soldiers: Edmonds, p. xiv.

Chapter Two

PAGE

9–10   Women's place in society: Welter, p. 21; Clinton,
         p. 91.

10   The Shenandoah Valley volunteers: Blanton, p. 26.

10   Black enlistments: Hunter, p. 5.

12   Kady Brownell: Harper, pp. 49–50; Eggleston,
         pp. 130–133; Leonard, pp. 113–121; Moore,
         pp. 54–64.

13   Marie Tebe: Leonard, pp. 150–151.

14   Susie Baker King: Harper, pp. 367–368; Taylor,
         p. 61.

14–15   Emily: Leonard, p. 239.

15–16   Sarah Emma Edmonds: Dannett, pp. 13–20.

16–18   Martha Parks Lindley: "Romance of an Ohio
           Woman"; Blanton, pp. 31, 40, 43.

18   Fanny Wilson and Nellie Graves: Eggleston,
           pp. 55–57.

18–19   Melverina Elverina Peppercorn: "Women Soldiering
           as Men"; Blanton, pp. 33–34, 38.

19–22   Malinda Pritchard Blalock: Harper, pp. 36–39;
           Stevens, pp. 33, 51, 54, 69, 97, 149.

23   Sarah Rosetta Wakeman: Burgess, pp. 1–13, 42.

23–25   Jennie Hodgers: Davis, pp. 108–112; Clausius,
           pp. 380–387.

25   Loreta Janeta Velazquez: Harper, pp. 395–396.

25   Charlotte Hope: Blanton, p. 41.

Chapter Three

PAGE
27   "Oh! If only" and "ashamed to let": Dawson,
           p. 120.

28   Women's dress: McClellan, pp. 476–480.

28   "A single glance": Leonard, p. 205.

29   "I am over eighteen": Catton, p. 40.

30   "You have pretty good health": Wiley, *The Life of
           Billy Yank*, p. 23.

30   Sarah Emma Edmonds: Dannett, p. 52.

30–31   Women in the enlistment process: Blanton,
           pp. 28–29.

31–33   Loreta Janeta Velazquez: Velazquez, pp. 52–69.

34   "We never undress": Blanton, p. 47.

34–35   Women adopting a male personality: Davis,
             pp. 110–111.
36–38   Frances Louise Clayton: Eggleston, pp. 39–40;
             Blanton, p. 52.
38   Melverina Peppercorn: Blanton, p. 53.

Chapter Four

PAGE

42–43   Gambling in camp: Wiley, *The Life of Johnny Reb*,
             pp. 38–39.
43–46   Rosetta Wakeman: Burgess, pp. 21, 22, 25, 31, 44,
             46, 48, 55, 58.
47   "Three divisions": Edmonds, p. 12.
47   Battle commands: Wiley, *The Life of Billy Yank*,
             p. 68.
48   "The sharp rattling": Velazquez, p. 101.
48   Exchanging items: Catton, p. 44.
48–49   Realities of military life: McPherson, p. 9.
50   "I have seen enough": McPherson, p. 33.
50   "The Twenty-fourth Ohio": Wiley, *The Life of Billy
             Yank*, p. 69.

Chapter Five

PAGE

56–57   Rebecca Peterman: "Another Female Soldier"
             (*St. Paul Pioneer*); "A Female Soldier."
57–58   Iron Brigade movements: Haskell.
58–60   Mary Galloway: Oates, pp. 91–93, 97–98, 381.

60   The movements of Baldy Smith's 6th Corps,
               2nd Division: Sears, p. 249.

62–64   Catherine E. Davidson: "Remarkable Incident."

64–65   The Battle of Antietam and "In a second the air":
               McPherson, pp. 3–5, 117–131.

65–66   Ida Remington: "Another Female Soldier" *(Fincher's
               Trades' Review)*; Herek, p. 1.

66   "For four miles" and "long mounds of earth":
               McPherson, p. 5.

66   The unknown Confederate woman: Blanton,
               pp. 91–92.

66–68   Sarah Emma Edmonds: Dannett, p. 195; Edmonds,
               pp. 162–163.

69–71   Clara Barton and Mary Galloway: Sears, p. 306;
               Oates, pp. 91–93, 97–98, 381.

71   Lincoln's proclamation: McPherson, p. 139.

Chapter Six
PAGE

73–74   Mary Scaberry: Blanton, p. 92.

74   Frank Martin: Eggleston, pp. 60–61.

74–77   Sarah Emma Edmonds: National Archives
               Administration, pension application files;
               Eggleston, pp. 23–31; Blanton, pp. 98–99.

77   "a corporal was promoted": de Pauw, p. 149.

79   Mary Ann Clarke: Eggleston, pp. 58–59.

79–80   Frances Hook and Mary Jane Green: Blanton,
               pp. 96–97, 82–83.

80   Andersonville: Eggleston, pp. 5–11.

80   "a filthy zoo": Blanton, p. 79.

Chapter Seven

PAGE

83   Rutherford B. Hayes: Perry, p. 187.

84   Rosetta Wakeman: Burgess, p. 57.

84   Rebecca Peterman: Blanton, pp. 152–153.

84–86 Mary Ellen Wise: Blanton, pp. 93–94.

86–87 Albert D. J. Cashier: Clausius, pp. 170–176.

87   Cashier tombstone: Durrant, p. 195.

87   Maria Lewis: Blanton, pp. 67, 174.

87–88 Martha Parks Lindley: Blanton, p. 166.

88–89 Elizabeth Finneran: National Archives
          Administration, pension application files; Blanton,
          pp. 164–165.

89   Lucy Gauss: Hoar, pp. 10–12.

89–90 Frances Clayton: American Antiquarian Society.

90   Sarah Emma Edmonds: Dannett, pp. 234–235;
          Edmonds, p. xxiii.

90–92 Loreta Janeta Velazquez: Harper, pp. 395–396;
          Blanton, pp. 176–183, 260.

93   "In our youth": Perry, half-title page.

A Civil War widow mourning her husband. This hand-colored lithograph, "The Soldier's Memorial," was published by Currier and Ives around 1863.

ILLUSTRATION CREDITS

★ ★

The illustrations in this book appear courtesy of the following institutions and individuals:

Abraham Lincoln Presidential Library: 86
American Antiquarian Society: 91
Archives of Michigan: 76, 77
Arnold Collection, U.S. Army Military History Institute: 12, 98
Boston Public Library, Boston, Massachusetts: 36, 37
Crawford Collection, U.S. Army Military History Institute: 24
Larry Eggleston, Wanatah, Indiana: 88
J. S. Hoar [first published in *The South's Last Boys in Gray*]: 89
Library of Congress: 2, 3, 6, 14, 26, 29, 40, 46, 52, 58, 60, 63, 64, 65, 67, 70, 72, 78, 80, 92, 94, 108, 110
Minerva Center, Inc. [from Burgess, *An Uncommon Soldier*]: 44
Museum Services, Gettysburg National Park: 13
National Archives, Washington, D.C.: 45, 85
National Park Service: 82
North Carolina Collection, University of North Carolina
　　Library at Chapel Hill: 21
Rhode Island Historical Society: 17
U.S. Army Military History Institute: 61
Wisconsin Historical Society: 56

Laundress in the camp of the 31st Pennsylvania Infantry.
Albumen print, 1862.

INDEX

★ ★

Note: Page numbers in **bold type** refer to illustrations.

Anita Silvey became "an armchair Civil War buff" while researching her own family history. When she first read about the existence and exploits of women soldiers, she realized she had to start afresh, learning about the Civil War from the perspective of the women who fought in it.

Ms. Silvey is among today's foremost authorities on children's literature. She is the author of several reference books on the subject for adults, among them *Children's Books and Their Creators*. A writer, teacher, and lecturer, she lives in the Boston area and travels widely both to promote her books and to emphasize the importance of high-quality books for children. *I'll Pass for Your Comrade* is her first book for a young audience.